CAL RIPKEN, JR.

Beating the tag of Chicago's Carlton Fisk, Cal is safe at home in a 1986 game at Memorial Stadium.

CAL RIPKEN, JR.
Quiet Hero

by
Lois Nicholson

TIDEWATER PUBLISHERS
Centreville, Maryland

The photographs in this book are reproduced through the courtesy of the following: Rich Riggins, frontispiece; AP/Wide World, pp. 3, 55, 66; Gil Dunn, p. 7; Vi Ripken, pp. 10, 13, 15, 16, 21, 24, 27, 46, 48, 74; Tim Norris, pp. 33, 36, 39, 45; Ted Patterson, pp. 56, 68, 71, 73; Scott Wachter, pp. 65, 85; Photo by Scott Wachter/1993 Tufton Group, Inc., pp. 79, 82, 88, 93, 94, 95; Bob Miller, pp. 86, 90, 92; *The Orioles Gazette*, pp. 77, 91; R&R Sports Group, p. 89.

Cover photograph by Scott Wachter/1993 Tufton Group, Inc.

Library of Congress Cataloging-in-Publication Data

Nicholson, Lois
    Cal Ripken Jr., quiet hero / by Lois Nicholson. — 1st ed.
      p.   cm.
    Includes index.
    ISBN 0-87033-445-X
    1. Ripken, Cal, 1960-   —Juvenile literature.   2. Baseball
players—United States—Biography—Juvenile literature.
    3. Baltimore Orioles (Baseball team)—History—Juvenile literature.
    I. Title.
GV865.R47N53   1993
796.357 ′ 092—dc20
[B]   93–22741
                                              CIP
                                              AC

Manufactured in the United States of America

First edition, 1993; third printing, 1994

CONTENTS

*Baseball is continuous, like nothing else
among American things, an endless game of
repeated summers, joining the long generations
of all the fathers and all the sons.*
—Donald Hall

To Double X, and to all children who are
searching for heroes.

FOREWORD

Cal Ripken was born with baseball sense. I watched him grow up. From the age of eight he was shagging flies in the outfield and taking infield practice. If he got in the way they had to kick him off the field.

You get a lot of kids who are the offspring of players or coaches, who just kind of fool around or like to hang around with the players and get autographs. They think that's real cool. What struck me about Cal was his love of playing the game and not just fooling around. He was never awestruck by all of it. Sure, he was impressed, but in his own quiet way. He was very shy but very observant. He watched and listened. I think he knew even in those early years that he wanted to be a baseball player. He was good at other sports, but like a lot of ballplayers, he just wanted to play baseball. There is something about it that gets to you. I was that way, and so is Cal.

Whenever I ask Sparky Anderson about some player or manager, if he really likes them, he'll say, "He has that look." Cal had that look from the time he was a kid.

Over the years he has changed very little. He still works as hard as anybody, harder than most. Never lets down. Still quiet, although he has become more adept at interviews. Still a leader by example. Always a gentleman, respected by everyone.

Not many people really know Cal Ripken. This book will help his fans of all ages to know him a little better.

—Rex Barney

PREFACE

When I was a child I was always delighted to find just the book I was looking for in our tiny library in Sudlersville, Maryland. Now, as a school librarian, nothing gives me more pleasure than to be able to answer children's requests for books by reaching for the shelf and handing them the very book they're looking for.

Several years ago, I began to hear the request, "Do you have a book about Cal Ripken, Jr.?" Alas, I had none. There was no such book. I began to think, "Someone should write a book about Cal." Finally, I simply decided to do it myself.

Why do so many students seek a book about Cal Ripken, Jr.? I see that children are searching for heroes, that they need someone to look up to, someone to respect.

As Cal closes in on Lou Gehrig's record of 2,130 consecutive games, there is irony to be found in the similarities between these two players. Lou Gehrig was a gentleman, respected by all, a quiet hero. Cal Ripken, Jr., is the same. Gehrig believed he belonged in the lineup every day. So does Ripken. Gehrig never stopped working to be a better player. Neither does Ripken. It is appropriate that in December 1992 Ripken received the Lou Gehrig Memorial Award as the major leaguer who best fits the image and character of the Hall of Fame first baseman.

What makes Cal a hero? Is it the way he conducts himself on and off the field? Is it his proud, confident, yet humble, manner? Is it his dedication and dependability? Or is it all of these?

I hope the reader will find the answers to these questions in this book. I also hope that this work will remind us that quiet heroes are heard above the crowd.

For their invaluable assistance with this book, I wish to thank the following: Vi Ripken; Johnny Oates; Larry Sheets; Tim Norris; Jimmy Williams; Rick Dempsey; Bob Miller and Rick Vaughn of the Baltimore Orioles; Greg Schwalenberg of the Babe Ruth Museum; Rex Barney; Chuck Thompson; Donnie Morrison, former Aberdeen High School baseball coach; Steven Batchelor; Dan Dierker; Calvin Morris; Frank Shriley; and Laurie Shillingburg of the Tufton Group, Inc.

© The Topps Company, Inc.

"UNBELIEVABLE"

I want to be remembered as an ironman . . .
—Cal Ripken, Jr.

Cal Ripken was worried as he stepped into the batter's box at the Toronto SkyDome for the home run–hitting contest on July 8, 1991, one day before his ninth straight All-Star Game. Cal usually avoided slugging contests. He believed that going for the fences might lead to poor hitting habits, which could trigger a batting slump. These slumps had plagued him throughout his career. Going into the All-Star Game, however, the thirty-year-old star shortstop for the Baltimore Orioles was in no such slump. He was leading the league with a .348 average, including 18 home runs, and he felt he must participate in the contest.

Cal took the first two pitches delivered by Toronto coach Hector Torres. On the third pitch, he lined a drive to center that smacked a billboard 430 feet away. Following a liner to left field, Cal's next blast almost scalped a vendor in the second deck in left-center. His next swing reached the third deck, a *mere* 450 feet away. Looking like a high liner over shortstop, Cal's next blow kept sailing until it cleared the wall. His fifth shot slammed into the foul pole on the third-deck level.

The American League dugout was alive with amazement. As Cal's teammates watched in disbelief, he put another one into the second deck at 420 feet. When Torres delivered the eighth pitch, Cal propelled his seventh hit out of the ballpark.

After two more swings, Cal headed for the dugout. But the crowd of 44,731 demanded more, and the stadium announcer, spontaneously abandoning the rules, sent Cal back to the plate. He lined another one into the stands, followed by two more shots, each more than 400 feet. Deciding to "dig down deep" for his final swings, Cal hit perhaps the longest ball of his life. It crashed into the

Cal won the home run contest by hitting 12 into the seats at the 1991 All-Star Game in Toronto.

fourth deck, at least 475 feet away, and landed within a yard of Jose Canseco's 1989 playoff blast, the only fifth-deck home run ever hit in the SkyDome.

With two final swings, Cal smacked a ball off the left field wall and completed the day with a second-deck drive that just hooked foul. It was over. Twelve home runs on 22 swings. The public address announcer declared, "The Cal Ripken Hour. What an exhibition!"

"Unbelievable," said Kirby Puckett. "Unbelievable," said Carlton Fisk. Even Cal described his feat as "unbelievable." Puckett lamented that Cal had ruined the contest for everyone else in it: Cecil Fielder, Howard Johnson, Danny Tartabull, and Bobby Bonilla. No one wanted to follow that act. "I didn't know what I was doing, but I didn't want it to stop," said Ripken. "I felt like a little boy."

Cal had to follow his own act the next day at the 62nd All-Star Game. If his performance during the home run contest was unbelievable, it mirrored an equally unbelievable career. As he took the field for his eighth straight start in an All-Star Game, he was enjoying his finest season. However, all of Cal's accomplishments during his ten remarkable years as a Baltimore Oriole seemed to pale by comparison to his best known achievement, "The Streak."

Going into the All-Star Game in 1991, Cal Ripken, Jr., had played in an astounding 1,491 consecutive games, second only to the legendary Lou Gehrig's record of 2,130. Gehrig was known as "The Iron Horse." Cal, a legend in the making, was already tagged "The Ironman."

President George Bush and Canada's prime minister Brian Mulroney were among the 52,383 spectators at the sold-out classic on July 9. Baseball greats Joe DiMaggio and Ted Williams were honored in pregame ceremonies.

The American League team entered the '91 contest with three consecutive victories over the National League, but going into the third inning, the National League led 1 to 0. With two men on base, Cal stepped into the batter's box to face a former Orioles teammate, Dennis Martinez of the Montreal Expos. In the first inning, he had singled to center. Martinez unleashed a waist-high slider on a 2 and 1 count. Cal connected. A fan sitting 416 feet away in the second deck caught a souvenir ball, and the American League moved ahead, 3 to 1. "I threw a slider that stayed up," said Martinez. "You don't make mistakes like that, especially to Cal, now that he's in some kind of a groove." When the evening was over, the American League All-Stars had their fourth consecutive win over the National League, 4 to 2, and Cal had the All-Stars' Most Valuable Player Award.

Dennis was right; Cal was in a groove, a golden groove etched into a golden season. At its conclusion, Cal had a .323 average with 34 home runs. It seemed only fitting for Cal to enjoy such success in the Orioles' final season at Memorial Stadium on 33rd Street where the Birds had played since 1954. Having spent his entire major league career in that stadium as an Oriole, Cal became the last Oriole ever to bat there, when, at 5:07 P.M. on October 6, 1991, he bounced into a 5-4-3 double play off Detroit's Frank Tanana.

Before the start of the season, much criticism had been leveled at Cal following his poor 1990 performance when he hit .250. People were saying he was tired and the pursuit of "The Streak" was preventing him from resting. Cal was the subject of much naysaying. However, the critics ate humble pie at the end of 1991 when Cal won his second American League Most Valuable Player Award, becoming the twentieth player to win multiple MVP awards and joining the ranks of such immortals as Stan Musial, Joe DiMaggio, Jimmie Foxx, Mickey Mantle, and Frank Robinson. This achievement was even more remarkable because he was the first player in American League history to receive the award while playing for a sub-.500 team. Next his critics had to swallow Cal's winning his first Gold Glove Award as well as being selected Major League Player of the Year. With their mouths so full of humble pie, the critics were silenced.

Cal's golden season crowned his meteoric rise in professional baseball. From the day he left the minors to join the Orioles in August 1981, Cal had climbed steadily until he reached the ranks of the game's all-time great players. He represented all that a professional athlete should be.

Lou Gehrig (left), the "Iron Horse," holds the record of 2,130 consecutive games that may be broken by Cal Ripken in 1995. Maryland slugger Jimmie Foxx (right), nicknamed "Double X," was a Hall of Famer and three-time American League MVP.

Cal was born into a baseball family. His father, Calvin Edwin Ripken, Sr., had spent his entire career with the Orioles organization, first in the minor leagues as a player and manager, and then as a major league coach and manager who made baseball history by managing both Cal, Jr., and his brother, Bill. Recalling his childhood, Cal, Jr., said, "I always had the hunger to play that all kids have, but it was more than that. When my dad went to coach in Baltimore, my favorite time was after the game. I was like a reporter. I'd review game charts and have all my questions ready. Why did the guy steal? Why didn't the catcher throw on this play? I would fire the questions at my dad. He'd tell me why everything happened. I'd question the player the next day. Why did you do that? What were you thinking? My bedtime stories were about foul tips splintering up fingers, and taping them together, spitting a little [tobacco] juice on them and saying to the umpire, 'Let's play.'"

A keen observer, Cal watched and studied and practiced. When he made it to the majors, he continued the same work habits that had helped him climb the countless rungs to reach the top. Orioles manager Johnny Oates told a baseball writer, "Cal hasn't missed an infield or batting practice in ten years."

Early in his career, Cal said, "I want to be remembered as an ironman, a player who went out there and put it on the line every day. I want people to say they couldn't keep him out of the lineup." This was Cal's quest from the beginning, and he was making it happen—play after play, inning after inning, game after game, and season after season.

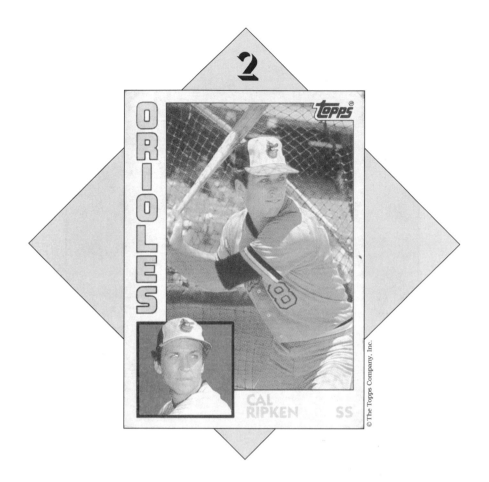

© The Topps Company, Inc.

TEETHED ON BASEBALL

Cal was born with baseball sense.
—Rex Barney

Calvin Edwin Ripken, Jr., was born in Havre de Grace, Maryland, on August 24, 1960. The Ripken family, which included one-year-old Ellen, lived in nearby Aberdeen, not far from Memorial Stadium where the Orioles played. Far away from his family's home, Cal Ripken, Sr., was enjoying his best year as a catcher for the Orioles minor league team in

*Four little Ripkens; from left: Ellen with baby Bill on her lap,
Cal, and Fred.*

Appleton, Wisconsin, in the Midwest League.
When news of his son's birth reached Ripken
in Topeka, Kansas, he asked manager Earl
Weaver for time off to be with his wife, Vi.
Weaver was reluctant to lose his catcher,
who was hitting .281, for even a few days,
but he agreed. Later he recalled, "It paid to
give him the day off."

Born and reared in Aberdeen, Cal, Sr.,
and Violet met in high school where she played

softball. They were married in 1957, the same year Ripken began his career as a catcher with the Orioles farm team at Phoenix, Arizona, in the Class C Arizona-Texas League. He had a good arm and could make the long throw to second base. Baseball ran deep in the Ripken family; Cal, Sr.'s older brother, Bill, had been an outfielder in the Brooklyn Dodgers organization.

"My brother Bill was a great two-strike hitter," Cal, Sr., told a writer. "I used to get upset with him when we were kids in semipro ball because he knew he could hit with two strikes, but I didn't know it. He'd surprise me. He knew what he wanted up there [at the plate]."

On a salary of $150 a month and $3 a day meal money on the road, there was not enough money for Vi to be with her husband during the season. She remained in Aberdeen and worked as a clerk for an insurance company to save the money to join him the next year in Wilson, North Carolina.

By the age of twenty-five, Cal, Sr., had made little progress toward playing in the big leagues. In Daytona during the '61 season, a foul tip smashed into his upper arm, bruising the deltoid muscle and knocking it out of alignment with the bone. The injury ended his ability to make the throws to second base and killed his chances of reaching the major leagues. He became a player-manager at Leesburg in the Class D Florida State League.

Vi Ripken's life centered around moving the Ripken family to wherever baseball took them. Small wonder then that when Cal, Jr., wrote a brief autobiography while in the sixth grade at Hall's Cross Roads Elementary School in Aberdeen, he stated, "My father's occupation, baseball, requires a lot of travel and so before I was a year old, we journeyed to Daytona Beach, Florida; Thomasville, Georgia; Little Rock, Arkansas; Leesburg, Florida; and Rochester, New York."

When Cal, Sr., returned to Appleton as a player-manager in 1962, his last active year as a player, Vi joined him with three little Ripkens in tow: Ellen, three; Cal, two; and six-month-old Fred. They rented an apartment over a store a few blocks from the ballpark. That summer Cal and his sister consumed large amounts of popcorn at the ballpark while Fred slept in his mother's arms.

One day Vi noticed a lump on little Cal's foot. The doctor she took him to said it was athlete's foot and prescribed some purple pills that were to be dissolved in water for soaking the foot. A few evenings later, while his parents were carrying some groceries into the kitchen, Cal climbed onto the table and put some of the pills in his mouth. "When we saw his purple mouth, we thought he had swallowed them," his mother recalled. "We took him to the hospital to have his stomach pumped." It turned out that he had not actually swallowed them, but for a while he had a purple mouth, a sore tummy, and two frightened parents.

In 1963 the Ripken caravan traveled from Aberdeen, Maryland, 1,500 miles to Aberdeen, South Dakota, for the summer. On a rare evening off, Mr. and Mrs. Ripken hired a babysitter and went out. When they called to check if everything was okay, the babysitter said calmly, "Yes, but Calvin was running around the room and tripped and fell and his head went through the wall." Fortunately, his head hit between the studs. "It didn't hurt me," Cal wrote, "but . . . it sure scared the babysitter."

Ellen coaches Cal on his pitching mechanics.

The following year, the Ripkens returned to Aberdeen, South Dakota, where some of the players Cal, Sr., managed were future Orioles Jim Palmer, Andy Etchebarren, Dave Leonhard, and Eddie Watt. By now, the three-year-old Cal had made up his mind he wanted to be a ballplayer.

"He always had a ball and a glove in his hands," his mother said.

While other kids ran around and paid attention to everything except the game, young Cal began his lifelong study of baseball. But it was not easy to concentrate on the action at the Aberdeen ballpark.

"It was always hot and the mosquitoes were terrible," he wrote. "They fogged the ballpark every day in an effort to get rid of the mosquitoes, but we still had to bring our cans of Off so we could watch the ball game without getting eaten up."

Assessing the performance of his father's team, he reported, "The mosquitoes didn't seem to bother the ballplayers, for they clinched first place two weeks before the season ended and my father was voted manager of the year."

Not content to study the players from the grandstand, Cal took advantage of his father's position by going onto the field during practice for some firsthand experience. One of his heroes at Aberdeen was the future Orioles shortstop, Mark Belanger. "This four-year-old kid was always out on the field, asking me to roll the ball to him," Belanger recalled.

Cal had a bat and ball in his hands before he was three.

As the years passed, Vi Ripken became an expert in the gypsylike routine of the baseball wife. She could store the furniture and pack the trailer in one day, make a huge batch of egg salad sandwiches, and take off for Georgia or Texas or South Dakota or wherever the trail took them. For Vi each year seemed to consist of repeated housecleaning cycles: go to spring training, rent an apartment, clean it, move a month later to wherever her husband was managing, rent an apartment or house, clean it, and return to home base four months later for the winter. Cal, Sr., often remarked that life is a series of adjustments and readjustments; Vi knew exactly what he was talking about.

Young Cal soon learned to appreciate how well his mother performed her role: "I guess it takes a special lady or special person to be a baseball wife," he told a reporter, "and she fits the mold perfectly."

Fred, Ellen, and Cal bury brother Bill in the sand at the beach.

In 1965, when the family followed Cal, Sr., 3,000 miles from spring training in Thomasville, Georgia, to the Tri-City team in Kennewick, Washington, Vi had four little Ripkens to take care of (Bill had arrived on December 16, 1964).

The cross-country trek was long and tiring since the interstate highways of today had not yet been built. There were thousands of miles of dusty two-lane roads to navigate, and the three older children fretted that the Easter Bunny would miss them in the wilderness of west Texas. But somehow dawn and the Easter Bunny found them in a Lubbock motel.

Cal learned more than baseball and survival on the road during these early travels. On the way home at the end of the season, the family visited Yellowstone Park, the Badlands, and Mt. Rushmore. The children even had their pictures taken with a native American woman, but Cal wrote that "Fred didn't because he was afraid and locked himself in the car."

After six years of life on highways and in ballparks, young Cal found the confinement of a schoolroom to be an unsettling experience. His first day of school in Aberdeen, Maryland, was "the worst day of my life," he wrote. ". . . I was always looking for a way out of the school. One day my teacher, Mrs. St. Pierre, went out of the room and I picked up my belongings and headed out the door, but my gym teacher, Mrs. Cruit, caught me." It was nothing personal against Mrs. St. Pierre, whom he liked, he added.

During those early years, the Ripken children grew very close. Every summer they were separated from their school friends, and in many of the towns they went to, the ball players were so young that there were no other baseball families. So they became their own best friends, and whatever they played became a real contest: Ping-Pong, volleyball, bowling. A love of sports and fierce competitiveness seemed to be born in all of them, but it was young Cal who had been dealt the largest portion of both.

"Most of the time I had to be the best," he told a reporter. "On the rare times somebody . . . beat me, it used to make me so mad. It seemed they were ganging up on me. If they ever beat me at anything, the whole house would hear about it. I didn't like that."

His mother agreed that, no matter what the game was, Cal had to win. "He wasn't in it for fun."

According to Orioles manager Johnny Oates, Cal's competitive nature is just as strong after ten years in the major leagues. "Everything is a game, a competition to him," Oates said. "I wouldn't want to be his kid. He might play checkers with his child and get the kid upset because she didn't crown him soon enough."

Indeed, the game of checkers proved to be one of Cal's earliest competitive encounters. "I split my head open playing checkers once," he recalled. "I was six and playing against the girl next door. I set her up for a five-jump move. She fell for it, I won the game, leaped up and banged my head on a concrete windowsill. I needed stitches."

Cal was not the only athlete in the family. His sister, Ellen, often expressed the belief that, if she had been a boy, there would have been three Ripkens playing in the big leagues. She played third base on a women's fast-pitch softball team that went to a national tournament. Even Cal conceded that she had the best arm in the family. Filled with pride as he watched his daughter playing softball, Cal, Sr., said, "Be damned if she didn't backhand a ball and throw it right over the top. She rifled that seed. I asked myself, 'Now where did she learn to do that?' I'd been teaching my players that for years and here I am sitting watching my own daughter do it better than anybody."

According to Cal, his brother Fred could have made it to the big leagues also, but never pursued sports seriously. "Maybe Fred got too much of it [baseball]," said Cal. "He wanted other things in life."

From 1966 to 1972, whenever school was out, Vi Ripken packed the family and the egg salad sandwiches and drove to wherever Cal, Sr., was managing: Aberdeen, South Dakota; Miami, Florida; Elmira, New York; Rochester, New York; Dallas-Fort Worth, Texas; Asheville, North Carolina. The desire to be a ballplayer did not grow in young Cal during these years; it had always been there. As he grew older, he became a more serious student of the game.

"Cal was born with baseball sense," says Rex Barney. But Cal also had the opportunity, as the son of the manager, to watch good players, to talk to them, and to ask them how they did things. Two future Orioles, Al Bumbry and Doug DeCinces, played at Asheville during those years. Before a game, third baseman DeCinces would work with him, answering his endless questions. During the game Cal sat in the stands, pretending he was Al Bumbry when the left-handed hitter was at the plate, then DeCinces as a right-hander. While other kids wandered around, he studied what the pitchers were throwing and how the infielders positioned themselves. After the game he quizzed his father on the moves he had made.

Cal lived in the world of minor league baseball. When Cal dreamed of playing baseball, he did not envision himself as a major league player. His heroes, Bumbry and DeCinces, were not yet big leaguers, and he did not see them beyond what they were, professional ballplayers in the minor leagues. That was all.

"It's funny," he later said, "but I never thought much about the big leagues like a lot of kids do. You know how most kids pick their heroes, play in the backyard, and pretend they're at the plate like some big league player? Well, for me it was different."

Cal almost didn't live long enough to realize his dream. One day when he was eleven, he was working out at McCormick Field with the Asheville team. Suddenly, from across the street, someone started shooting randomly at the field with a rifle. A shower of bullets

Vi took Fred and Cal to the ballpark in Aberdeen, South Dakota, in 1964 to watch their father at work.

whizzed by the players on the field. At first they were stunned and bewildered, then they started diving for cover. With bullets kicking up the dirt in front of him, Doug DeCinces grabbed Cal by the arm and threw him into the dugout. "I'll never forget it," DeCinces said. "That's how close it was."

No charges were ever brought against the shooter and no one ever solved the mystery, but the incident has become a permanent part of Cal Ripken's story.

Although Cal had few opportunities to watch the Baltimore Orioles in action before his father became a scout in 1975 and then a Baltimore coach in 1976, Cal saw enough of third baseman Brooks Robinson to adopt him as a big league hero. Robinson recalled watching Cal growing into adolescence. "He was always around the ballpark. He lived and died baseball. I know guys are supposed to like baseball, but some are special. It's almost a sin if they don't play. The thought of not playing every inning never crosses their minds. That's the way the game is meant to be played. That was young Cal."

ATTRACTING THE SCOUTS

Don't Take Me Out
—Cal Ripken, Jr.

While young Cal crisscrossed the country and hung around minor league ballparks with his father's team, he also put down roots long enough to play Little League, Babe Ruth, and Mickey Mantle League baseball. Copying his dad, who outshone the stars on the field as Cal's number one hero, he began at twelve as a catcher in Asheville. But he soon abandoned

Cal's first Little League team in Aberdeen, Maryland. Cal is fourth from left in the back row.

the position, preferring to pitch and play the outfield.

His dad rarely saw Cal play, even through his high school career. "Baseball took my dad away from me," Cal told a writer. "He left at one o'clock every day on the days he was at home, and he was gone completely half the time, on the road. I learned very early that if I wanted to see my dad at all, I would have to go to the ballpark with him."

Hoping to spend time with his father, Cal accompanied his dad to the ballpark. "He'd put me in a uniform and send me to the outfield and say, 'Don't come into the infield, Son. It's too dangerous in there. You can get hurt bad. Shag flies or whatever. And always keep your eyes open.'" Cal recalled, "I still wouldn't get to see him that much, but I'd ask questions on our drives to and from the ballpark. I liked those drives."

It was Vi Ripken who took her son to baseball practice and to games, who parked her lawn chair behind the home plate screen, and, armed with a thermos of Kool-Aid, offered parental support and encouragement. "She's a special lady," Cal told a reporter. "She was there for me."

Like all parents, Cal's mother wanted Cal to know she was rooting for him. "You sit there and don't want to yell when your kids are playing," she said. But sometimes she got carried away and her voice filled the infield.

Cal was a tough competitor from the start. One day he was pitching and he hit three or four batters in a row. The coach walked out to the mound to try to settle him down, but quickly returned to the bench. Laughing, he said to Vi Ripken, "When I got out there, your son just looked at me and said, 'They don't get out of the way very fast, do they?'"

Cal got his first taste of victory in 1973 at the age of thirteen when the Asheville Little League team won the state championship and went to the southeastern regionals in Florida. But that was as far as they got. "That was the biggest thrill of my life," he wrote in his eighth grade essay.

That fall Cal played soccer on a youth league team in Aberdeen, which his father coached. He quickly learned that he would be treated as just another player. "Dad did everything in a professional manner. I remember being embarrassed when he got into me for goofing off," Cal said.

At fourteen, Cal was a runty 5-foot, 7-inch, 128-pound freshman at Aberdeen High School when he went out for the baseball team in 1974. On the first day of tryouts, coach Donnie Morrison asked the group of fifty boys to run a mile in under 6 minutes, 30 seconds. Some dropped out before they got a quarter of the way; others lagged far behind.

"One little kid came up to me," Morrison recalled. "He was all red in the face and panting. In this high-pitched voice he said, 'Coach Morrison, I just can't do it today. May I come back tomorrow and try again?' That was the first time I saw Cal Ripken."

It was unusual for a freshman to make the varsity team, but timing was on Cal's side. The team had lost many veteran players to graduation, so Cal won the second baseman's spot.

"Everyone called him Calvin in high school," Coach Morrison said. "From his earliest days, Calvin's presence on the field was exceptional and he had gifted hands when it came to fielding ground balls."

Up against pitchers who were bigger and threw harder than he was used to, Cal later

Cal was a pitcher-shortstop for Aberdeen High School.

confessed to feeling a little scared. He struggled at bat, hitting less than his weight. He batted ninth and got a lot of practice putting down sacrifice bunts.

The next year Cal had grown a few inches and added about 20 pounds to his frame. No longer intimidated by bigger players, Cal had an early opportunity to demonstrate his tenacity in a game against Elkton High School. One Elkton player, Steve Slagle, stood 6 feet, 5 inches, and weighed 270 pounds. Slagle was on first base and came roaring toward second. Cal, playing shortstop, came over to cover. Slagle lowered his shoulder and slammed into Cal's ribs, knocking Cal ten feet into the air.

Coach Morrison ran out to him. Lying on the ground gasping for breath, Cal begged, "Don't take me out."

Morrison ignored the plea and took him out, but high school rules allowed a player to reenter the game, so before it was over, Cal was back in the lineup.

During that season Baltimore scout Dick Bowie first saw Cal, but he was not impressed. "To be honest, I went to the game to see a player on another team," Bowie said. "I paid absolutely no attention to him other than the fact I knew he was Cal, Sr.'s boy."

In the eleventh grade Cal grew to be 6 feet tall. He continued to play shortstop, but he also began to pitch for Aberdeen. His father was now a coach for the Baltimore Orioles, and Cal had an opportunity to observe major league pitchers and ask questions. He had learned to throw a curve and slider and change-up, and was far ahead of other high school pitchers and hitters.

His pitching drew the attention of the hordes of bird dogs (part-time scouts) and full-time scouts. Dick Bowie of the Orioles was now impressed. "He'd be playing shortstop and all the scouts would be standing around and waiting for him to come in and pitch," Bowie said. "I was hoping they wouldn't put him in so they wouldn't see just how good he was."

Baseball was not the only sport Cal played in high school. He earned two letters in soccer, was the team captain, and made all-county and all-metro teams.

In 1977, with Cal pitching, the Putty Hill Optimists team from Baltimore made it to the Mickey Mantle League World Series in Sherman, Texas, but they lost the series.

Cal's mother never missed a game, her lawn chair a fixture behind the screen back of home plate. On at least one occasion, his brother Bill cut classes in middle school to watch Cal pitch. For the first few innings, he hid behind a tree so his mother would not see him. When it was time for him to be there legitimately, he appeared at his mother's side. "How's he doing?" he asked.

"He walked a guy," she said.

"No, he didn't," Bill said, before he could catch himself.

Cal didn't let his sports activities interfere with his schoolwork. In the classroom, as well as on the playing field (or the checkerboard), he strived to be the best. His favorite subject was math, and he did not duck the tough courses, choosing to take calculus as an elective. He graduated with a 3.5 average.

Cal credits his parents with teaching him the difference between right and wrong, and what kinds of situations to avoid. Even when he disagreed with their advice, he did not rebel, but went along with it. "That's not to say I was always a great kid," he told a writer. "Sometimes I disobeyed and misbehaved, but for the most part I believed and respected my mother and father."

By his senior year in 1978, Cal had grown to 6 feet, 2 inches, and 185 pounds. He was now the bigger kid that smaller freshmen hitters feared. He won 7 and lost 2 with a 0.70 ERA, striking out 100 in 60 innings. A 1978 scouting report for the Texas Rangers stated: "Built like and has Jim Palmer–like actions . . . pitches well . . . good poise and savvy . . . only 17 . . . should be faster . . . recommended signing bonus $20,000."

Never one to sit out a game, Cal played shortstop when he didn't pitch. Being an everyday player appealed to him more than being a pitcher. Always the first on the field and the last off, Cal worked long hours on his hitting. Asked to describe Cal in one word, Coach Morrison chose, "Focused. He knew what he wanted to do, and he was able to do it."

During batting practice the Aberdeen team played a game called 3 and 2. As long as a hitter did not take the count beyond 3 balls and 2 strikes, he could continue to hit. "Cal never missed," Morrison said. "They had to make a special rule, limiting him to 15 hits."

Cal batted .492 in his senior year to win the Harford County batting title, and he drove in 29 runs in 20 games. But his hitting was incidental to all the scouts except Dick Bowie. When Cal pitched a two-hitter and fanned 17 for the Aberdeen Eagles to win the Maryland Class A championship game 7 to 2 over Thomas Stone High at Prince George's Community College, he became a hot prospect on many major league draft lists—as a pitcher.

But many scouts believed that the Orioles had the inside track on Cal because of his father's long service in the Baltimore organization. In fact, Cal himself preferred to play for the Orioles, but he could not control how the draft would go. The Orioles liked him as an infielder, but were willing to let him decide if he wanted to be a pitcher instead. One week before the June 6, 1978, free agent draft, Cal worked out privately at Memorial Stadium.

The Orioles, who had gained three extra picks because of the loss of players to free agency, chose a third baseman from Cincinnati, Bob Boyce, as their first-round selection. In the second round, they picked Larry Sheets, an outfielder, and Ed Hook. Then, for their regular selection in the second round—the forty-fourth pick overall—they chose Cal Ripken, Jr. (Boyce and Hook never made it to the major leagues).

The Orioles were in California that day. When he heard the news, Cal, Sr., called his wife. "Today we had a son drafted," he said.

"Oh, I've known it would happen for months," Vi quipped.

Cal's father had seen him play maybe one game a year for the past ten years; his mother had seen him develop while the hordes of scouts swarmed around him.

A week later, the Orioles signed Cal for a bonus of $20,000 and $500 a month, the standard salary for first-year minor league players. On the same day, they signed Tim Norris, a pitcher out of Archbishop Curley High School in Baltimore, giving him an $18,000 bonus. Both players could earn additional bonuses as they moved up from Rookie League to the majors.

On the morning of June 14, Cal, Sr., drove his oldest son to Archbishop Curley High School where they met Tim Norris; his mother, Emily Norris; and Tim's high school sweetheart and future bride, Chris DePazzo. Bidding his father farewell, Cal, Jr., got into Tim's beige Monte Carlo and the four headed for Bluefield, West Virginia, home of the Orioles Rookie League farm team, to begin training for the June 22 start of the Appalachian League season. Geographically, Bluefield was less than 400 miles from home, but in many ways the two rookies were entering a whole new world, the world of professional baseball.

*Cal with Tim Norris, relaxing on Tim's beige Monte Carlo
that got them to Bluefield.*

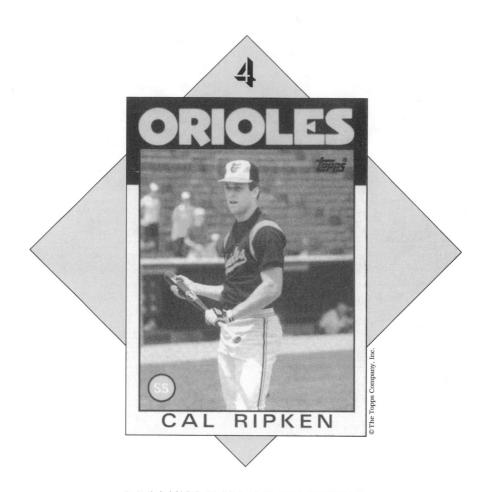

BREAKING IN AT BLUEFIELD

It was the most fun I had in baseball . . .
—Cal Ripken, Jr.

For most young ballplayers, the move from amateur to professional is a jolting adjustment, and Cal was no exception. Like most players who are drafted in the first few rounds, he had been the leader, the star, the big guy in high school. When he arrived in Bluefield, he suddenly became just one among twenty-five players who were just as good or better.

Ralph Rowe, Bluefield batting coach, understood what they were going through. "For the first time in their lives, they are feeling pressure," he said. "They never knew what pressure was before. All along, they were playing the game for fun. They were always the best on their team so they didn't have to worry. But now they are playing for money and everyone here is as good as the next man. They are constantly looking over their shoulders if they make a mistake."

Many Orioles favorites of the past, including Don Baylor, Boog Powell, Bobby Grich, Mark Belanger, Doug DeCinces, and Eddie Murray, started out in Bluefield. But the harsh reality was that fewer than one in ten who started there would ever play a game in the big leagues. As focused and confident as young Cal was, he was "scared to death" that everybody else would be better than he was.

Cal had one advantage over the other rookies at Bluefield: he knew what life in the minor leagues was like. The years of following his father to bush leagues all over the country, watching how players handled things and how they lived, left him with no questions about life in the minors. He was prepared for the all-night bus rides over winding mountain roads after a night game. He was not surprised to see players sleeping on stacks of sweat-soaked uniforms or in the overhead luggage racks on the ancient bus. He felt as if he had been on the road every summer for the first twelve years of his life. Many rookies who were away from home for the first time suffered

A pair of pinball wizards, seventeen-year-old rookies Cal Ripken and Tim Norris in Bluefield, 1978.

attacks of homesickness that distracted them from concentrating on playing the game. Cal's Bluefield teammate, Larry Sheets, recalled, "Cal stood out from the rest of the rookies. Because he had been around baseball all his life, he possessed a maturity we didn't have. He knew the lingo. He also knew how to separate the fun side of baseball from the business aspect of the game."

Bluefield was a coal mining town of about 16,000 inhabitants, nestled near the south-western border of Virginia. Orioles manager Johnny Oates, who began his career as a catcher there in 1967, remembers the town fondly. "Their slogan is: 'The city in the moun-tains—you don't need an air conditioner,' and it was true. It felt like fall all summer, very cool. Bowen Field, where the Baby Birds played, was set in a hollow of the mountains; the sky beyond the center field fences was filled with a big green mountain."

The so-called clubhouse was a step down from the facilities at Aberdeen High School. "Each player had a tiny cubicle," Oates said. "They were little screened-in lockers, and you had to take your uniform out to have room to hang up your clothes. There wasn't room for both."

Players had to wait their turn to use the few showerheads. There was a tunnel from the clubhouse to the dugout, but very few players used it. The ceiling was only 5 feet, 10 inches from the floor; to avoid bumping their heads, most players went out the back door and walked around the clubhouse to get to the field. A fence along the third-base line was often decorated with laundry hung out to dry in the cool mountain air (in the Appalachian League, the players did their own laundry). The lights on the field were sparse and were not turned on until it was almost pitch black, to save money.

When Tim Norris and Cal Ripken arrived in Bluefield, their first objective was to find a place to stay. They quickly teamed up with two other newcomers, Mike Boddicker, a twenty-year-old pitcher from Norway, Iowa, and Larry Sheets, eighteen, from Staunton, Virginia. Together, the four rookies rented the two second-floor bedrooms at Ilee Short's boardinghouse. Mrs. Short, a seventy-year-old widow, told the ballplayers they couldn't be any more trouble than the teenaged girls she had been boarding. The rookies paid $25 a week each for their rooms, two meals a day, and laundry service.

There was not much social life in Bluefield. The players spent their free hours playing cards or billiards, and talking baseball. Life in the minors was twenty-five young men from all over the country living and working together day and night for two and a half months. At the end of the season they considered each other brothers; there was such a strong sense of camaraderie. With nothing to spend their money on, Tim and Cal managed to save some of their $500 a month salary and $6.50 a day on-the-road meal money.

General manager George Fanning presided over every aspect of baseball at Bowen Field. When he wasn't answering the phone,

Cal and Tim reach the second rung in the Orioles' ladder at Miami in 1979.

"Ballpark," he might be found stocking the concession stands, hanging out the laundry, selling tickets, mowing the outfield grass (he was also the groundskeeper), or repairing the bleachers. For twenty years Fanning was a familiar sight at Bowen Field, regally attired in oversized khaki pants that hugged him below his oversized waistline, a cigarette constantly dangling from his lips. When it came time to carry the batting cage on and off the field, Fanning whistled for his "grounds crew"—the players. In 1993, he began his thirty-fifth season at Bowen Field.

The week before the season opener was filled with hours of drills on fundamentals: bunting, fielding, turning the double play, baserunning, hitting the cutoff man, learning to play the game the Orioles' way. At every rung on the Orioles' organizational ladder, from the minor leagues up, Cal found the routine always to be the same. Cal had decided he preferred to play every day and gave up all ambitions of being a pitcher. Each man eyed the others to see where he fit on the talent scale. Coaches jumped on every mistake made by the nervous rookies, adding to the pressure each youngster was putting on himself. Of the twenty-five players on the Bluefield roster, more than half were still teenagers.

"A normal reaction for a kid coming into pro ball is to be a little confused and scared," Rowe said. "After all, you have five or six coaches running around telling you all the things you are doing wrong. All of a sudden a kid will begin to think, 'If I'm doing so many things wrong, why did they sign me? I'm not doing anything right.'

"But the difference between the amateur and the pro is the little things . . . Very few times will you find these things in a kid you sign . . . so we have to teach him from scratch."

In the minor leagues, the role of the manager is primarily teaching. He has to know how each player will react to instruction, and what it will take to help each individual improve. Cal's first manager in pro ball, Wilbert "Junior" Miner, knew that "some players would respond best to a pat on the back, and others would only go with a kick in the butt." Tim Norris recalled Junior Miner as a patient, fatherly, hardworking man of slight build who was always quick to give a word of encouragement.

Cal made his professional debut on June 22, 1978, but he was no instant superstar. During the first fifteen games of the season, he made so many errors at shortstop, many people were wondering why he had been picked so high in the draft. He was hitting below .200. When these questions took the form of verbal gibes from the stands, they shook Cal's confidence. The average attendance at Bluefield was about 400; some brought their own chairs and sat, talking among themselves, near the foul lines. But every seat was close enough to the field to make every catcall plainly heard. The fans peppered Cal with "Go back to Little League," and "Ripken, hit the ball for a change." At the end of the season Cal admitted, "After all those mistakes, I was scared."

For a while he played better away from Bluefield. He was totally focused on learning and improving. With the help of Ralph Rowe and Junior Miner, Cal made some adjustments and began making plays he had missed earlier. His hitting improved, too. Playing in 63 of the 70 games, he finished with a .264 average and 24 RBIs. He did not hit a single home run.

Despite the primitive ballpark facilities, the long bus rides, and his sputtering start,

Cal enjoyed his professional baseball debut. Looking back ten years later he recalled, "It was the most fun I had in baseball because we were all the same. As you go up and up, it gets to be more of a job." And Cal was climbing up and up on the rungs of the professional baseball ladder.

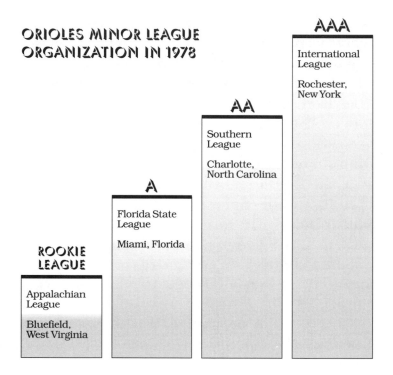

ORIOLES MINOR LEAGUE ORGANIZATION IN 1978

AAA
International League

Rochester, New York

AA
Southern League

Charlotte, North Carolina

A
Florida State League

Miami, Florida

ROOKIE LEAGUE
Appalachian League

Bluefield, West Virginia

Cal played for every team in the organization before reaching the Orioles.

CLIMBING THE RUNGS

Nobody ever heard him cry, "Enough."

Cal Ripken moved up just one rung on his climb to the major leagues when he went to Miami in the Class A Florida State League in 1979. Still growing and adding weight, he hit .303 with 28 doubles and 5 home runs in the five-month season. His fielding also improved sharply, and he was named the all-star short-stop for all Class A leagues. But, in fact, he played more than half the season at third base.

Oddly, he became a faster runner as he gained weight and power. Scouts who had clocked him going from home to first in 4.5 seconds in high school, now observed him covering the distance in 4.2 seconds.

When the short Florida season ended six days before his nineteenth birthday, Cal was called up to Charlotte in the Class AA Southern League. The first time he took batting practice in Charlotte, the ball seemed to be leaping off his bat over the fences. That inspired him to swing for the fences every time he got into a game, and in fact he did hit 3 home runs in 17 games. But he made only 8 other hits and struck out 13 times. That taught him a lesson: concentrate on meeting the ball and the home runs will take care of themselves.

Cal reported to Charlotte in 1980 as a 6-foot, 4-inch, 205-pound nineteen-year-old. That height and weight were unusual dimensions for a shortstop, the position requiring quickness and agility more than power. In spring training Cal never counted the ground balls he fielded, or the number of times he practiced getting a jump to steal a base. Coaches could hit hundreds of ground balls to him and run him all day. Nobody ever heard him cry, "Enough."

On May 8 at Jacksonville he smashed a gigantic three-run home run over a 40-foot wall. When he hit a game-winning home run in the eleventh inning the next night, he felt for the first time that he belonged. "What you don't realize when you're in the minors is that

A far cry from Camden Yards, Tim and Cal at Bowen Field in the Appalachian League.

you're being molded all the time. By AA ball it seems to fit and make sense. That's the biggest jump there is—from A to AA. That's when you start seeing 3 and 2 breaking balls and 2 and 0 change-ups."

Cal had carried the self-imposed burden of proving that he was not in the Orioles organization just because of his father. Cal knew a lot about the game—he had been studying it since he was five, but the most important thing he knew was that he still had a lot to learn. When he fell into a slump, he did not hesitate to call his father; long distance calls took a big bite out of his minor league pay. "I'd tell him I was hitting grounders to short and without even seeing me he'd say something that worked."

Cal was a third baseman at Rochester when he was called up to the Orioles at the tail end of the 1981 season.

Cal was usually even-tempered, but even gentle giants have their limits. On a hot sticky 96-degree night in July in Charlotte's Crockett Park, the "caring, respectful" Ripken, as manager Jimmy Williams described him, got ticked off. After John Shelby's two-run homer gave Charlotte a 4-2 lead in the fourth, Ripken was the next batter. Sending the next batter sprawling in the dirt with a well-aimed pitch after a home run has been hit is an old baseball custom, one that Ripken had no interest in continuing. When the Memphis pitcher threw one near Cal's head, Ripken charged the mound. According to a Charlotte writer, "It started a riot that even Attila the Hun wouldn't have jumped into without reinforcements." Cal came out with a few scratches and bruises—not enough to put him on the sidelines. He played every game and made the All-Star team at third base.

What caught the Orioles' eyes more than anything was Cal's emergence as a long-ball hitter; he hit 25 home runs and 28 doubles while batting .276. A low-ball hitter with power, he had gone to the plate each time aiming to drive the ball and pull doubles down the line. He did not know if the 25 home runs were a fluke.

Eager to prove that he could handle even better pitching, Ripken played winter ball in Puerto Rico, where he faced major league caliber hurling. He batted .279 with 6 homers and 38 RBIs in the short season, and was named MVP of the pennant-winning Caguas team.

Cal was named MVP of the Caguas club of the Puerto Rican League after the 1981 season.

Cal went to spring training in Miami in 1981 with the Orioles, who considered him their best prospect since Eddie Murray. A shoulder injury sidelined him for a week, during which his father observed, "If the kid can't work, they'll need chains to keep him down. He'll go nuts not being able to take his swings."

He did have time to read his winter press notices, which touted him as a surefire American League rookie of the year in 1981. But every time he started believing them, he looked out and saw Doug DeCinces firmly in charge of third base.

Many organizations would have promoted the twenty-year-old infielder to the big team anyhow, on the strength of his three minor league years. But the Orioles' way has always been to bring players along slowly. In twenty years only two players had skipped the AAA level on their way to the top: Dave McNally and Jim Palmer. For another year of experience and learning, the Orioles sent Cal to Rochester, New York, in the AAA International League, where his father had been a player and manager. Baltimore manager Earl Weaver's parting words to him were, "See you soon."

At Rochester, Cal started out like a Babe Ruth, blasting 3 home runs in one game on April 27, and two 3-run shots a month later. Playing 85 games at third base, he occasionally filled in at shortstop for Bobby Bonner, the Orioles' top shortstop prospect.

On Saturday, April 18, Ripken spent his longest night in baseball. At Pawtucket, Rhode Island, the Red Wings and Red Sox commenced play at 8 P.M. After 9 innings, the score was 1 to 1; both teams scored again, but not until the 21st inning. After 8 hours, 7 minutes, and 32 innings, the game was suspended at 4:07 Easter Sunday morning, tied at 2 to 2. Of the original crowd of 1,740 fans present on Saturday night, only 20 were still there at the end. The game resumed when the two teams met again on June 23. Pawtucket scored a run in the 33rd inning to win the longest game in baseball history both in time and innings. Cal had become a part of baseball history.

The tougher the pitching in Class AAA ball, the better hitter Ripken became, batting .288. His 23 home runs and 31 doubles proved to him and everybody else that his big year at Charlotte had been no fluke. Those early years of studying pitchers and asking questions in minor league parks all over the country seemed to be paying off. He called himself a "guess hitter," but Red Wings manager Doc Edwards explained, "He doesn't just guess up there. He can figure out a pitcher's pattern."

Midway through the season a sportswriter noted, "Ripken is probably no more than a half-season away from a lifetime of first-class hotels, cross-country flights, and megadollar contracts."

Meanwhile, for most of June and July there was no major league baseball, because the players went out on strike. When club owners considered bringing up minor league players to replace striking big leaguers, Cal made it known that he would not go if asked. But when the strike ended on August 8, the Orioles promoted him to Baltimore. Cal and his dad would once again ride together to Memorial Stadium for each home game.

Cal made his big league debut on August 10, 1981, against Kansas City, when Earl Weaver sent him in to run for Ken Singleton, who had doubled. One batter later, John Lowenstein singled, and Cal raced home from second with the winning run. He made his first base hit off Chicago's Dennis Lamp on August 16. He played a few games at short and third, and pinch-hit four times, unsuccessfully. His last plate appearance on September 11 left him with a .128 batting average.

For the last three weeks of the season he sat on the bench and watched, except for two appearances as a pinch runner. And he did not like it. "It was eating my insides out," he said later. "I told myself, 'If you get a shot to play, don't come out.' When you think about it, that's what baseball's all about—playing every day. You can only play so long. A lot of players seem to have some kind of regrets when they're finished. I want to do what I can while I can."

Cal Ripken, Jr.
ORIOLES • THIRD BASE

© Fleer, Inc.

"THE STREAK"

I've seen a lot of players who remind me of other players,
but I've never seen one like Cal.
— Joe Altobelli

At the beginning of the 1982 season, everybody in Baltimore was expecting big things from Cal. During the winter he had played for the Caguas club in the Puerto Rican League, and one reporter wrote this about him: "The word from Puerto Rico on Cal Ripken is that he's hitting everything in sight. That includes his own teammates. Ripken slammed a car door on Bill Swaggerty's thumb forcing the pitcher to return to Baltimore for x rays." Cal led the league with 49 RBIs and was named MVP.

There were some significant changes in the Orioles lineup that year. They had traded their third baseman, Doug DeCinces, to the California Angels for outfielder Danny Ford. Shortstop Mark Belanger had signed with the Los Angeles Dodgers as a free agent. With both positions on the left side of the infield open, manager Earl Weaver, who planned to retire at the end of the year, gave the third base spot to Cal.

On April 5, the Birds opened at home against the Kansas City Royals. Dennis Leonard was on the mound for the Royals when Cal stepped into the batter's box for his first at-bat in the second inning. Ken Singleton was on base when Leonard hung a pitch over the plate. Cal connected with a line drive that cleared the wall for a homer. Recalling the shot, Cal said, "I could hardly believe it, and I didn't go into a home run trot. I almost jumped into the air and then went around the bases. Singleton was just jogging around in front of me and when he got to home plate I was right behind him." Cal followed the homer with two hits and the O's won the game 13 to 5. "That's when I really started to feel like a big leaguer."

Ten years later Cal said, "If I had to pick out the most exciting day of my career, it would be the opening day of my rookie season in 1982 . . . I can't ever remember being as nervous as I was at that time. There were

50,000 people in the stands, and my family was there, with my father coaching at third base as usual."

Cal's opening day fireworks were short-lived as he immediately slid into a deep slump. Even for a player raised around baseball, the pressure of the big leagues can be overwhelming. "Sometimes it all got to me—the triple-deck stadiums, the media, the whole major-league atmosphere," Cal said. "It was mostly mental. I began worrying about things other than the actual game. Everything compounded it. I got a big buildup in Baltimore. All of a sudden I started thinking they were expecting me to hit all those home runs."

Feeling the pressure to perform, Cal repeated one of his minor league mistakes of "going for the fences" each time at bat. "I started to use an uppercut swing because home runs were expected of me," he remembered. "Then, every day I didn't get a hit, my confidence sank lower and lower. It was starting to get to me. I was trying so many different stances, taking everybody's advice, and getting confused."

Getting advice from everyone, Cal became increasingly frustrated until Reggie Jackson offered him a timely comment. One day, while Earl Weaver argued with an umpire, Reggie Jackson, waiting on third base, said to Cal, "Hey, I want to talk with you. I know you can play. Just go out there and do what you can do. Do what got you to the big leagues, and everything will take care of itself." Jackson's

Present Hall of Famer Joe Morgan steals second under the glove of future Hall of Famer Cal Ripken, Jr., in the 1983 World Series.

words sank in, and Cal realized that he had to go back to the basics.

During the '82 season, Cal established a strong relationship with Eddie Murray, the Orioles first baseman who batted fourth behind Ripken in the lineup. "In my first season, when I was slumping, Eddie helped me. When he came up [to the majors] and didn't know any of the players, he had felt out of place, so he knew what I was going through."

By May 1, Cal was 7 for 60 in 18 games. On May 2, he stepped in to face Seattle pitcher, Mike Moore. Moore delivered a fastball that Cal saw coming at his head. Too late to dive for the dirt, Ripken turned his head. The ball hit Cal, opening a lemon-sized hole in the back of his helmet. Cal lay

Eddie Murray encouraged the rookie Ripken during an early slump in 1982.

sprawled across the plate. Manager Weaver ran from the dugout and Cal, Sr., raced in from third. Determining he was not seriously hurt, Weaver and the trainer led him off the field. Relieved that he was not injured, someone later joked that at least he had gotten on base for a change. As he had done as a high school sophomore, Cal asked to be allowed to remain in the game, but Weaver sat him down. Many players who are hit in the head by a pitch never fully regain their hitting form, but the beaning did not affect Cal; in fact, it may have snapped him out of his slump. He missed only one game after that and hit .281 from May 2 to the end of the season, showing that he was not gun-shy at the plate.

By the time Cal began facing pitchers for the second time in the major leagues, he was outthinking them. A student of the game since his youth, Cal became an excellent judge of pitchers as he studied their habits and patterns, tried to read their minds, and often accurately predicted their pitches.

On May 29, 1982, Cal suited up for a doubleheader against the Toronto Blue Jays, starting at third base in the first game. Weaver replaced Cal for the second game with Floyd Rayford. It was the last game in which Cal did not start for eleven years through the end of the '92 season.

In late June, high-level discussions raged within the Orioles organization regarding the shortstop position. Bobby Bonner was hitting a poor .169, and Earl Weaver wanted a strong bat in the lineup. The Baltimore skipper wanted to move Cal to shortstop, but many thought Cal, at 6 feet, 4 inches, too tall for the position. There had never been a regular major league shortstop so tall in the history of the big leagues. Weaver argued, "Ripken's got hands as good as Brooks Robinson and Mark Belanger. And his arm is as strong as Aurelio Rodriguez's."

[In the 1850s, the position of shortstop was originally called the "short fielder." At that time, all second basemen played very close to their bases. Because most batters were right-handed, the space between second and third had to be filled. Later, the term was changed to shortstop when, in the 1860s, the "short fielder" was positioned to "stop" ground balls from going through the infield.]

On the afternoon of July 1, Cal strode into the clubhouse unaware of the discussions about the Orioles shortstop position. Glancing at the lineup taped to the wall, Cal was stunned to see a 6 beside his name, indicating the shortstop position, instead of the usual 5 for third base.

"I thought Earl made a mistake. He hadn't prepared me for the move," Cal recalled. He consulted his father who gave this no-nonsense advice: "Don't worry, just catch the ball and throw it to first base."

Weaver instructed Cal, "I just want you to catch the ball, take your time, and make a good throw. If he's out, he's out. If he's safe, he's only on first base."

Cal quickly adjusted to his new position and soon came to prefer shortstop over third.

He was later quoted in *Baseball Digest* as saying, "You can't afford to take a step back at third. You have to be like a hockey goalie. There's some fear. There's no comfort zone. You're on edge. It's a highly stressful, anxious position."

Following Cal's move to shortstop, his offensive efforts improved as well. The Orioles also came alive. From August 10, the Birds went 33-10 down the stretch to challenge Milwaukee for the championship of the Eastern Division. Going into the final four games of the season, the Orioles were three games behind Milwaukee. The Orioles, facing the Brewers in Baltimore for a weekend stand, swept a doubleheader on Friday night and won again on Saturday. Baltimore's season ended on Sunday when Milwaukee rebounded behind the bat of Robin Yount whose 4 hits secured a 10 to 2 Brewers' victory. It was manager Earl Weaver's last game.

Cal won Rookie of the Year honors for the 1982 season as he led all major league rookies with 28 home runs and 93 runs batted in.

Joe Altobelli took over as manager of the Orioles in 1983. Cal settled into his second full year in the major leagues. Never a socializer, he explained his daily routine: "I did not like to be sidetracked during the season; I think I'd give up almost anything to play baseball. I'd have something to eat and get to bed around one A.M. Then the next day, I was up at eleven, had something to eat, read the papers, watched TV, ate again, and went to the ballpark. I got to watch 'Ryan's Hope,' 'All My Children,' and 'One Life to Live,' but

'General Hospital' got cut off because I had to get to the ballpark."

Beginning the '83 season with a strong performance, Cal received an invitation to play in his first All-Star Game, which ended in the American League's first victory since 1971. Like most rookie All-Stars, he was awed by the event. "I felt good enough to be there, but I was looking around the locker room at guys I used to root for. You sit there and talk to yourself and say, 'Oh, God, how do I belong in this group?' and you say, 'I'm here, aren't I? I must belong.'"

Cal escaped a phenomenon known in baseball as the sophomore jinx. Many times, players who have enjoyed a big rookie season seem to slump in their second year, unable to maintain their early success. Some theorize that players who fall victim to the jinx were never really that good. Pitchers, familiar with hitters' habits, learn how to pitch successfully to them and if the "sophomore" cannot outthink the man on the mound, he is doomed. Others believe that on the heels of an outstanding first year, players often feel the pressure from the fans and the media and try to sustain the initial momentum. In the end, they lose their concentration and their confidence.

This was not the case for Cal. During 44 games, from August 13 through September 25, Cal hit .391 with 14 doubles, 9 home runs, 30 runs batted in, and 40 runs scored. The Orioles went 34 and 10 in that period and clinched the Eastern Division Championship. When Baltimore took the title in Milwaukee,

Cal, Sr., broke a twenty-seven-year self-imposed rule during the celebration that ensued, pouring a can of beer over Cal's head. "I guess the father in me finally came out," he admitted.

The Birds faced the White Sox for the pennant and won a trip to the World Series by taking three straight after losing the opener. Cal hit .400 to lead all hitters for both teams. The Orioles went on to defeat the Philadelphia Phillies in the Series, four games to one. In the fifth and final game, Scott McGregor hurled a shutout. Eddie Murray, awesome on offense, smashed two home runs in the 5 to 0 win. The final out came when Garry Maddox hit a drive to Cal who snared the liner as he grinned broadly.

But Cal's magnificent year was still not over. In addition to winning a World Series ring, he received the American League's Most Valuable Player Award. With customary humility, Cal said, "MVP is not something you aim for. By the same token, you want people to know about you. I like to be someone the kids would like to grow up to be like, to emulate in their backyard games. You have to be careful to be really good in their eyes. They model themselves after you.

"I hate to use the word fame and I hate the word celebrity. I'm not comfortable with that," said Cal of his quick rise to fame. "All this has not changed me. I don't act bigheaded and I have too many friends who would be the first to tell me if I did."

In contrast to Cal's humble summation of his magnificent 1983 season, Orioles manager Joe Altobelli said, "I've seen a lot of players who remind me of other players, but I've never seen one like Cal."

In Cal's lifelong study of baseball, he had developed wisdom beyond his twenty-three years. He observed the career highs and lows of many players, both from the vantage point of a child raised in the minor leagues and that of a young man climbing through the minors to the majors. He knew that it was hard to get to the top and even more difficult to stay there. Talking to columnist Tom Boswell, Cal defined his idea of a perfect baseball career: "I'd like to play every game, every inning, every day for twenty years."

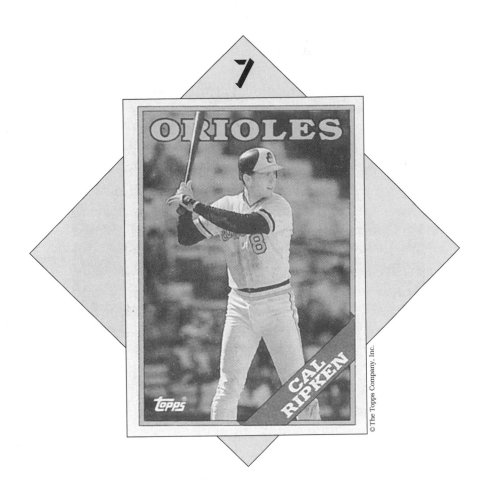

ORIOLES

CAL RIPKEN

Topps

© The Topps Company, Inc.

THE RIPKEN THREE

He doesn't put himself above anyone.
—Vi Ripken

At the beginning of the 1984 season, manager Joe Altobelli was asked what Cal could do to improve on his magical 1983 season. The skipper answered, "You don't expect anybody to improve on that kind of a year." However, Cal worked to improve his fielding—he had made 25 errors in 1983. "That's what I want to improve on this year, and cutting down on the number of balls I throw over [first baseman] Eddie Murray's head," he said. "I figure we either have to work on Eddie's jumping ability or my aim. Most likely my aim, because it's tough to catch a ball 12 feet over your head."

Cal signed a four-year, four-million-dollar contract with the Orioles before the 1984 season. Downplaying the contract, Cal said, "The satisfactions that you get from playing the game, from catching the last out of the World Series—those feelings are a lot greater than [signing a big contract]." Vi Ripken, proud of her son's humility, said, "I'm proud of the way he handles himself. It makes you feel like you've done a good job. He doesn't put himself above anyone. He's part of us everyday people." His father said, "That young man isn't going to change. When they see Cal bust his fanny all the time like the other twenty-four guys, they'll forget all about the money."

Realizing the importance of being an active community citizen, Cal donated 2,000 free tickets to disadvantaged children in Harford County, Maryland; provided the services of a physical therapist for a day care center for children with disabilities; and pledged his support to the Baltimore School for the Performing Arts.

Cal continued to perform well in the '84 and '85 seasons, hitting .304 and .282. His defensive performance improved.

Three Ripkens together on the same team.
From left: Bill, Cal, Sr., and Cal, Jr.

While Cal always worked hard, he also enjoyed pranks and horseplay. Rick Dempsey, the veteran Orioles catcher, recalled Cal rooming with Floyd Rayford. "Cal loved to wrestle. He was a prankster, high-spirited, full of energy, and he did not know his own strength. Cal would hide in the room, then jump out and ambush Floyd, or he would wake him up by turning the bedding over onto the floor with Floyd in it and jump on him."

Dempsey roomed with Cal during the '83 and '84 seasons. During a trip to California in the winter of '84, Rick tried to spark Cal's interest in surfing and boating, but Dempsey's efforts were in vain. It seemed that if Cal

"Cal has sure hands," says former Orioles shortstop Mark Belanger.

couldn't play catch on a boat, he wasn't inter-
ested. However, Dempsey and Ripken formed
a successful team of jokesters. "One of our
pranks was to booby-trap broadcaster Tom
Marr's room on the road. We would get hold of
a key to his room, go in and do things like
putting pine needles under the sheets, filling
a bucket with water and putting it on top of a
door so it spilled when he opened the door,
soaking his pillow, sticking his toiletries to the
bathroom counter with Super Glue, or putting
cellophane over the toilet seat. Marr may have
suspected Cal and me, but he could never
prove anything." Another time, in Seattle, the
dynamic duo found Marr asleep in a chair and
taped his arms and legs to the chair.

At the end of the '84 season, Cal had
played 4,064 consecutive innings. When asked
about taking a day off, he said, "I've been
playing all the time my whole career. I would
like to have the option to go up to Joe Altobelli
and tell him I need a day off. I've often thought
about that when I had some nagging injuries.
But when I can't help the team, when I can't
turn a crucial double play, then it's time to get
out of the lineup."

Early in the 1985 season, Cal's streak was
seriously threatened. On the second day of the
season in a game against the Texas Rangers,
Cal began to move toward second base for a
pickoff play against Gary Ward. "My spikes
got caught on top of the bag," said Cal, "I heard
a pop, felt the bang. I said, 'That's it. It's
broken.'" Luckily, he was mistaken. Baltimore
trainer Richie Bancells taped Cal's left ankle

Two superstars who worked hard to get to the top, and to stay there: Cal with George Brett of the Kansas City Royals.

and he returned to lead off the next inning. The following day, his ankle ballooned, but since the Orioles were playing an exhibition game with the Naval Academy, Cal was able to rest. "The Streak" remained intact.

In discussing "The Streak," Cal said, "The only streak involved is a season. I condition myself to play 162 games in a season. Then I rest up for the next year. I like to play. I don't like to sit."

The Orioles were mired in fourth place in mid-June of '85 when Joe Altobelli was fired as manager and Earl Weaver came out of retirement. Still struggling in '86, they lost 42 of their last 56 games and finished last for the first time since moving to Baltimore in 1954. But, off the field, 1986 proved to be one of Cal's most exciting years.

One evening Cal was eating in a restaurant when Joan and Robert Geer came in. Avid Orioles fans, the Geers noticed Cal, and Mrs. Geer asked for his autograph.

"Who should I address it to?" asked Cal.

"My daughter, Kelly," replied his future mother-in-law.

Proudly, Mrs. Geer gave the autograph to her daughter. Kelly, a six-foot-tall blond graduate of Dulaney High School and the University of Maryland, said, "That's great, Mom, but who is he?"

Two months later, Kelly and a friend were at a restaurant where Cal was appearing for a promotion. More than a hundred women surrounded him. When Kelly learned what all the excitement was about, she made her way through the crowd, tapped Cal on the shoulder, and said, "You met my mom and gave her an autograph for me. Thanks."

The two chatted briefly. Later, Cal called her and they dated. On New Year's Eve 1986, Cal invited Kelly to his home after dinner. He took her to the balcony where she saw the words "Will you marry me?" written in Christmas lights mounted on boards in the yard.

Cal and Kelly were married on November 13, 1987. Their daughter, Rachel Marie, was born November 22, 1989. (A second child is expected in July 1993.)

Another exciting event occurred on the day after the '86 season ended. Cal Ripken, Sr., became the manager of the Orioles. The Ripkens became the third father-son, manager-player combination in baseball history, following Connie Mack and his son, Earle, and Yogi Berra and Dale.

Reporters drilled Cal, Sr., with questions concerning his managing of Cal, Jr. With his customary frankness, the senior Ripken replied, "In managing fourteen years in the minor leagues, everybody was my son. You're a father, a guidance counselor, a bus driver, everything to those kids. Now this young fellow comes along who happens to be my real son. Well, so what? Our association on the field has always been professional. He knows my job and I know his."

Cal, Sr., had been with the Orioles for twenty years, on both the minor and major league levels. Known for his tough-as-nails manner, Cal, Sr., was respected by many for his knowledge and experience. Johnny Oates, who played for Cal, Sr., in the Florida instructional league, said, "I was and still am an early guy to get to the ballpark. Cal, Sr., is the one who taught me to get there early, because if you don't, someone's going to learn something you won't have an opportunity to learn."

Larry Sheets and Cal, who broke in together at Bluefield,
were teammates in Baltimore in the mid-1980s.

At twenty-seven, Cal, Jr., wanted to play
every game despite the inevitable injuries that
a major league ballplayer suffers. He learned
such toughness from his father, and recalled
a story that illustrated Cal, Sr.'s approach to
baseball and life. When Cal, aged sixteen, and
his brother Bill tried to help their father clear
the roads around their Aberdeen, Maryland,
home following a snowfall, their old tractor's
battery was dead.

"Dad starts to hand-crank it," Cal described, "and the engine backfires. The crank
flies up and opens a gash on his forehead and

I'm saying, 'Let's go to the hospital.' My dad says, 'Just go home.' He's got an oily rag held up to his head. He goes into the bathroom, slaps a couple of butterfly bandages on it, goes back out and starts the tractor and plows the snow off the road. That's my dad. That should make you understand a little."

The Ripken father-son duo became the Ripken father-sons trio on July 11, 1987, when Bill Ripken joined Cal, Jr., in the Orioles lineup. The brothers played side-by-side with Bill at second base and Cal at shortstop. [Only three other families have ever had three members in uniform on a major league team at the same time: Jose, Hector, and Tommy Cruz; Felipe, Matty, and Jesus Alou; and George, Sam, and Harry Wright.]

In August, Cal's streak reached 8,058 consecutive innings and 883 consecutive games, but Cal was deep in another slump. When someone suggested he take a day off, Cal replied, "It's an excuse; I don't want to hear it. When I'm not hitting everybody says, 'He's tired; he needs a day off.' I wonder what excuse they would use if I took a day off and still was in a slump." Commenting on the slump, coach Frank Robinson said, "There is no blueprint way to get out of a slump. Some guys rest, some forget taking batting practice. Others do like Rip: They play their way out of it."

Not only did Cal try to play his way out of the slump, he attempted to practice his way out of it by returning to fundamentals. Cal reported to Memorial Stadium in the early afternoon prior to every night game. He and his father set up a stationary tee. Cal would work off the tee, hitting the ball to all fields. He went back to basics and more hard work. Cal said, "You have to try not to put pressure on yourself. Build up your confidence by saying, 'I'm going to come through.' But you also have to accept the fact that though there are times you'll come through, there will be times when you won't. It's great when you do, but you can't get down on yourself too much when you don't."

Father and son talk baseball behind the batting cage.

Despite intense criticism from the media, Cal showed grace under pressure. His high school coach, Donnie Morrison, attributed Cal's poise to Cal, Sr. "Cal is able to deal with so many situations in baseball because his father taught him that baseball is a business and Cal is able to always keep that perspective."

Cal, Sr., demonstrated his managerial toughness on September 14, 1987, when he took his eldest son out of the game. It was the first time Cal had been pulled since June 4, 1982, and while his consecutive game record continued, his consecutive inning streak ended at 8,243. Not questioning his father's decision, Cal said, "It was a surprise [to be taken out], but I didn't feel I needed an explanation. The manager's job is to make the moves. It just so happens, in this case, that [the] manager is my father."

But even a gentleman occasionally loses his temper. Cal's usual calmness erupted during a game with the Yankees in Baltimore on September 25, 1987. He argued too long over a called third strike in the first inning, and umpire Tim Welke ran him from the game. It was Cal's first major league ejection.

Cal ended the 1987 season with a .252 average. The Orioles finished sixth in their division with 67 wins and 95 losses. The team hoped to improve their fortunes in 1988, but the Birds dropped their first six games and Cal, Sr., was fired. The senior Ripken returned

Bill and Cal went to spring training together for the first time in 1987.

to the organization the following year in his former spot as third base coach for his replacement, Frank Robinson. But the Orioles continued their slide, going 0 and 21 at the start of the season. Ultimately, the ailing O's lost 107 games.

In July Cal had signed a three-year, $6.2-million contract. He batted .264 for the seventh-place team.

"The Streak" continued through '88 and '89 and with each added game it received increasing attention. Teammate Randy Milligan said, "He has to do it every day. He can't come in like anyone else and say, 'Hey, I'm tired. I need a day off.' And he can't be hurt. It's got to be a big cast where there's no way he can play."

Cal's second thumbing [ejection] occurred on August 7, 1989, when Baltimore, playing at home, took on Minnesota. The two players at bat before Cal had been called out on strikes. When the first two pitches to Cal were called strikes, he quickly indicated his disagreement with the calls. What started out as a quiet argument quickly escalated. On-deck hitter Keith Moreland, Robinson, and Cal, Sr., restrained Junior, but not before umpire Drew Coble had thrown him out of the game. Coble later said, "That was the most miserable two and a half hours I ever spent, for a guy to put me in a situation like that. It was like running God out of Sunday School."

On August 17, in a game against Toronto at Memorial Stadium, Cal became the third player in the history of major league baseball

Kelly Ripken is actively involved in the couple's many community activities.

to reach 1,208 straight games, passing Steve Garvey's 1,207. The fans gave Cal a standing ovation.

The Orioles managed to finish second in their division in '89. Cal batted .257.

As Cal's baseball career continued to unfold, his role as a dedicated member of his community expanded. During the '89 season, Cal and Kelly Ripken contributed $250,000 to the city of Baltimore to establish an adult literacy program facility. Announcing the plans for the development of The Ripken Learning Center, Cal said, "Kelly and I have a need to put something back into the community that has been so good to us." The center, which opened in July of 1990, annually serves 240 students. In 1991, Cal established the Reading, Runs, and Ripken Program. It was based on corporate and other donations for each home run that he hit. His 34 roundtrippers raised $100,000 for the program that first year.

Cal joined his friend, Eddie Murray, in establishing a program that provided Oriole home-game tickets for disadvantaged residents of the Baltimore area. The Children's Center at Johns Hopkins Hospital and the Baltimore School for the Performing Arts received Cal and Kelly's support as well.

At the end of the 1989 season, Cal was named the first winner of the prestigious new honor, the Bart Giamatti "Caring Award." Created in honor of the late baseball commissioner, Bart Giamatti, who died on September 1, 1989, the award recognized Cal's contributions to the community.

"Cal represents baseball in the highest degree," said Orioles general manager Roland Hemond. "And when you talk about role models, you want your children to be like Cal Ripken is. To me that's always the supreme compliment."

Cal signs for fans during a break in spring training.

© The Topps Company, Inc.

BASEBALL'S "IRONMAN"

I just want to be recognized for baseball.
—Cal Ripken, Jr.

To be a major league ballplayer one must learn to stay the course amid the rough and smooth waters that accompany one's career. During the '90 season, Cal batted his all-time low of .250 for a full season and the Orioles did not fare much better. From 1986 to 1991, the Orioles lost more games than any other club in the majors.

On June 12, 1990, the public address announcer Rex Barney informed the crowd that Cal was playing his 1,308th consecutive game, surpassing Everett Scott's mark. Only Gehrig's "Iron Horse" record of 2,130 remained before him. But the fans, frustrated by the poor performance of the Orioles and Cal, greeted the news with a chorus of boos.

Cal's defensive performance remained strong despite his hitting slumps. He made only 8 errors in 1989. When he mishandled a ground ball on July 27, 1990, during the fifth inning against the Kansas City Royals, the bobble ended his streak of 95 errorless games and 431 chances without an error, both records for shortstops. Always watching and learning, Cal credited his mentor, Mark Belanger: "He always told me to watch the guy playing my position when I was sitting in the dugout. He always said, 'If that shortstop does something wrong, tell yourself you won't do that.' He also told me to keep my eyes on Alan Trammell. He felt Alan was one of the best ever. I thus got into the habit of checking other guys out. I still do that. I must also say that Belanger was a master of his position. His advice, his voice, come back to me all the time."

The Orioles showed little improvement at the beginning of 1991 and on May 23, Johnny Oates replaced Robinson, becoming the tenth manager in Orioles history. Like Cal, Oates had begun his career with the Orioles in Blue-field. Spending much of his career with the Orioles farm teams, Oates played for Cal, Sr., and had known Junior as a child. "In Miami, we played day games and I'd be there 8:00-8:30 A.M. As soon as I'd get my uniform on, here came this little six-year-old dirty faced kid, already soaking wet from the Florida sun. He loved to kick a soccer ball out against the

Cal's batting stance, which he adjusts from time to time.

center field wall and he'd come in with a soccer ball under one arm and a ball and glove in the opposite hand. 'Mr. Oates,' he'd say, 'let's have a catch.' Remember, it's only 8:30 in the morning, but I'd go out and play catch with him. Our careers started together that way and now here I was managing him.

"I didn't see Cal from the time he was a little boy until I was released by the Yankees on May 30, 1981, and went to Columbus in the International League as a coach. Cal was then an all-star third baseman in Rochester. The first time I saw him there I knew this guy was head and shoulders above everybody in that league. Not only his physical abilities, but the way he thought, the preparation he made to play. Most guys that age just get in there, see the ball thrown, and hit it. Not Cal. Before he stepped into the batter's box he'd stand there studying the pitcher: 'What is he going to throw me here . . . with this count and a runner on second, what is he going to try to do?' That was what I noticed about this now twenty-year-old. He'd grown up to want to use his brain to play the game as much as his physical abilities."

The Orioles continued to struggle under Johnny Oates, finishing sixth with a 67-95 record. But for Cal Ripken, Jr., 1991 was a super season. His .323 average, 34 home runs, and 114 runs batted in were career highs. He became the second player ever to win MVP, Player of the Year, All-Star Game MVP, and Gold Glove honors in one year (Dodgers' shortstop Maury Wills in 1962 was the other). No American Leaguer had ever been named MVP while playing for a sub-.500 team.

Opening day of '92 found the Orioles in their magnificent new home at Camden Yards. Continuing as the Orioles' first family, the three Ripkens, Cal, Sr., Cal, Jr., and Bill represented a total of fifty-three years in Oriole uniforms. While the beautiful new downtown ballpark received much attention in Baltimore and throughout the nation, all eyes were fixed upon Cal as well. On opening day, "The Streak" stood at 1,573. Cal's contract would end at the close of '92, and the press buzzed with speculation about the negotiations. Everyone knew Cal would draw a multimillion dollar contract, but questions arose about the Orioles' willingness to make a long-term commitment to a thirty-two-year-old player.

Cal ignored the media hoopla and, as always, quietly went about the business of baseball. Frequently asked about his contract, Cal replied, "There are two sides to baseball, the playing side and the business side. I try to take care of the playing side and leave the business side to my advisors."

On August 24, Cal celebrated his thirty-second birthday. The Orioles chose the occasion to announce their agreement with their star shortstop. Cal signed a five-year contract for $30.5 million. In addition, the club offered him $4 million to work for them at the end of his playing days. "We think Cal Ripken is a first-ballot Hall of Famer," said club president Larry Lucchino. "He personifies the best of the

Cal celebrated the signing of his new contract on his thirty-second birthday with (from right) his wife, Kelly, daughter, Rachel, and mother, Vi.

Baltimore Orioles organization, and we are pleased and proud that he will be performing for the organization for many years."

Up to the All-Star Game, Cal had been hitting at a normal pace for him, but he went into a lull after that, and closed the season with a disappointing .251, his second lowest average in eleven full seasons. But the Orioles, benefiting from a much-improved pitching staff, nipped at first-place Toronto's heels for most of the season before finishing third.

In November Cal was voted the American League's outstanding shortstop for the second consecutive year in a poll of the league's managers and coaches conducted by *The Sporting News.* Mike Hirsh, a recent graduate of The

Cal was the lone Ripken in an Orioles uniform as he warmed up on opening day, 1993.

Ripken Learning Center, presented the Gold Glove to Cal in a touching ceremony at Oriole Park at Camden Yards. "This was one of my most difficult and frustrating years," Ripken said, "but it makes me feel good that I was recognized and it gives me something positive to look back on as I move toward the 1993 season."

For the first time in his major league career, Cal Ripken, Jr., was the only Ripken on the Orioles roster when the team gathered for spring training in March 1993. During the winter the Orioles had released both Cal, Sr., and Bill. A free agent, Bill signed with the Texas Rangers.

The experience of being the lone Ripken on the first day in camp left Cal feeling "weird and saddened a little bit and disoriented." It seemed strange not to see his father on the coaching lines, and to look to his left and see somebody else working out at second base beside him. Anticipating the first time the Orioles would face the Rangers in an exhibition game, Cal told a reporter, "I never had to play against him . . . Now all of a sudden we're on separate teams . . . I just don't know how I'm going to feel or how I'm going to react." By the time the two teams met on March 28, Cal had had time to digest the changes. But it still felt strange for him to see Bill in another uniform.

Cal was too much the professional to let the breakup of his baseball family affect his performance. Aware that many observers blamed his '92 second-half slump for the Orioles' failure to win their division, he was determined to come back strong in '93. Asked if he thought he could return to the form that led to two MVP years, he said, "I know I can do it again. I don't know how you describe 'it,' but whatever it is, I feel like I have it. I feel very confident."

Thanks to a far-sighted schedule maker, the Orioles drew the Texas Rangers to open the 1993 season at Oriole Park at Camden Yards on April 5. The initial adjustments were harder for Bill. He arrived at the airport as a visitor to his own hometown, and talked to Cal on the telephone. The first time they saw each other was on the field—wearing different

On opening day, April 5, 1993, Bill Ripken of the Texas Rangers and Cal played their first game as members of opposing teams.

uniforms. But they had almost met accidentally. "I started to walk to the wrong clubhouse before I corrected myself," Bill said.

When the players were introduced to the crowd before the game, the Baltimore fans gave Bill the biggest ovation of the day, which made both brothers feel good.

In the Orioles dugout, Cal thought, "I had some weird feeling that maybe this was just a loan, and Billy would come back." But once the first pitch was thrown and the game began, reality set in. When Bill came up to bat, Cal plotted how to play him defensively with the same thoughtful scrutiny he gave every other hitter. When Cal came up with men on base, Bill was hoping he would not drive them in. Of the two, Bill enjoyed the day more; the Rangers won, 7 to 4. For Cal, it was game 1,736 of "The Streak," but the loss counted for more.

Although the Orioles got off to a slow start, losing their first three games, Cal's determination to do better than he had in '92 was quickly evident. He was 9 for 18 in the first four games.

As the '93 season got under way, the six-year-old kid with the dirty face remembered by Johnny Oates had grown to become a superstar, baseball's "Ironman." "He doesn't do it with a lot of flash," Oates said. "He

At the age of thirty-two, baseball's "Ironman" says he has come further than he ever thought he would.

doesn't run around high-fiving everybody. If he hits a home run, he goes around the bases like he doesn't want anybody to notice. He just plays the game. He is a superstar who wants to be treated as the ordinary person that he is. He wants to be looked at as being nothing special. But because he is a superstar, he can't be just Joe on the street."

Cal prefers to believe that he can remain the way he sees himself: ". . . the same as everybody else. I'm one of you guys in Baltimore," he said in a 1993 TV interview. "That's who I am. That's where I'm from. Nothing will change that."

He realizes, however, that he cannot escape being treated as a superstar, even in his

In 1993 the Cal Bar was introduced; royalties go to the Cal and Kelly Ripken Foundation to benefit the numerous charities the Ripkens support.

Cal enjoys a quiet moment at the ballpark with his daughter, Rachel.

own home. "Sometimes [my daughter Rachel] calls me 'Cal Ripken' and that's odd. I mean, she should call me 'Daddy' all the time. But she hears the name on TV or she watches the game on TV . . . you wish that you could control that."

When people talk about Cal Ripken, Jr., several defining words are heard again and again. The word "gentleman" is often evoked in describing Cal by people who know him. His high school coach, Donnie Morrison, said, "Cal has always wanted to be the same kind

This poster appeared in schools throughout Maryland.

of community citizen as Brooks Robinson. And Cal continues to be his own person. In this era when many players go unshaven, Cal is always neat and well groomed."

"Respect" is another word frequently used to characterize Cal. "Everybody respects Cal," said Rex Barney, "the media, players from other teams, everybody. A lot of players don't get that. They are nice people, but they don't carry respect."

"The one thing—the one word, is respect," echoed Johnny Oates. "Respect for his teammates, for his parents, for his fans, for his manager, that he has a responsibility, that we don't owe him anything. A lot of athletes today think that the world owes them something."

"If there is one thing I would like people to know about Cal," said Larry Sheets, "it's that he is unchanged, that with all the success he has achieved, he is still the same person that I first knew when we met in 1978 as rookies in Bluefield."

"Consistent" is another word associated with Ripken. His onetime teammate, veteran pitcher Mike Flanagan, said of him, "The thing about Cal is that he's always the same. Except, oftentimes, he's better than the same."

Brady Anderson, Cal Ripken, Jr., Mike Devereaux, and Chris Hoiles (left to right) *observe the action during the Orioles 1993 spring training in Florida.*

Cal goes into the hole and plants to make the long throw during spring practice.

Competitive . . . dependable . . . consistent . . . a gentleman . . . respect . . . unchanged—these are the colors of the palette used to paint a picture of Calvin Edwin Ripken, Jr., baseball's "Ironman." When asked how he would like to be remembered, the legendary shortstop slugger replied, "I just want to be recognized for baseball. I want to be known as a good ballplayer. I'd like it if there was some eight-year-old kid out there imitating my batting stance. That's what I always did. And I'd like to think that someday two guys will be talking in a bar and one of them will say something like, 'Yeah, he's a good shortstop, but he's not as good as ol' Ripken was.'"

When Cal can extend his arms and get around on the pitch, it travels far.

CHRONOLOGY

1960

Aug. 24—Born in Havre de Grace, Maryland.

1974

Makes varsity team at Aberdeen High School as a freshman.

1977

Pitches in Mickey Mantle World Series in Texas.

1978

Leads Aberdeen High to victory in regionals.

June 13—Signs with Baltimore Orioles.

June 22—Plays first professional game for Bluefield, West Virginia, Appalachian Rookie League.

1983

July 6—Plays in his first All-Star Game.

October—Plays in his first World Series.

Named American League Most Valuable Player (MVP).

1984

Sets American League record for assists by a shortstop (583).

1987

Cal, Sr., becomes manager and brother Bill joins the Orioles.

Sept. 14—Consecutive inning streak ends at 8,243.

Hits 20 or more home runs for tenth consecutive year.

Nov. 13—Marries Kelly Geer.

1989

Nov. 22—Daughter Rachel Marie is born.

Kelly and Cal Ripken donate $250,000 to the city of Baltimore for The Ripken Learning Center.

1979	1980	1981	1982
Plays for Miami in Class A Florida State League.	Plays in Charlotte, North Carolina, in Class AA Southern League.	Plays for Rochester, New York, in Class AAA International League. April 18—Plays in longest game in the history of organized baseball. August 8—Called up by Baltimore Orioles.	May 2—Beaned by Mike Moore. May 30—Begins streak of consecutive games played. June 5—Begins streak of consecutive innings played. Named Rookie of the Year.

1991	1992	1993	1994
Receives the first Bart Giamatti Award. Named American League MVP for second time. Wins his first Gold Glove.	Named All-Star MVP. Wins Roberto Clemente Award, as the player who best exemplifies the game of baseball both on and off the field. Wins second Gold Glove. Wins Lou Gehrig Memorial Award.	July 26—Son Ryan Calvin is born. Becomes top home run hitting shortstop in ML history. Leads AL shortstops in assists 7th straight year, tying league record.	Starts record 11th straight All-Star Game at shortstop. August 1—Plays in 2,000th consecutive game. At end of season, Cal's consecutive game streak stands at 2,009.

STATISTICS

YEAR	CLUB	AVG	G	AB	R	H	2B	3B	HR	RBI	BB	SO	SB	CS	HP
1978	Bluefield I	.264	63	239	27	63	7	1	0	324	24	46	1	1	2
1979	Miami	.303	105	393	51	119	*28	1	5	54	31	64	4	3	1
	Charlotte	.180	17	61	6	11	0	1	3	8	3	13	1	0	0
1980	Charlotte	.276	144	522	91	144	28	5	25	78	77	81	4	2	3
1981	Rochester	.288	114	437	74	126	31	4	23	75	66	85	0	2	2
	Baltimore	.128	23	39	1	5	0	0	0	0	1	8	0	0	0
1982	Baltimore	.264	160	598	90	158	32	5	28	93	46	95	3	3	3
1983	Baltimore	.318	+162	*663	*121	*211	*47	2	27	102	58	97	0	4	0
1984	Baltimore	.304	+162	641	103	195	37	7	27	86	71	89	2	1	2
1985	Baltimore	.282	161	642	116	181	32	5	26	110	67	68	2	3	1
1986	Baltimore	.282	162	627	98	177	35	1	25	81	70	60	4	2	4
1987	Baltimore	.252	*162	624	97	157	28	3	27	98	81	77	3	5	1
1988	Baltimore	.264	161	575	87	152	25	1	23	81	102	69	2	2	2
1989	Baltimore	.257	162	646	80	166	30	0	21	93	57	72	3	2	3
1990	Baltimore	.250	161	600	78	150	28	4	21	84	82	66	3	1	5
1991	Baltimore	.323	*162	650	99	210	46	5	34	114	53	46	6	1	5
1992	Baltimore	.251	*162	637	73	160	29	1	14	72	64	50	4	3	7
1993	Baltimore	.257	*162	*641	87	165	26	3	24	90	65	58	1	4	6
**1994	Baltimore	.315	112	444	71	140	19	3	13	75	32	41	1	0	4
ML Totals		.277	2074	8027	1201	2227	414	40	310	1179	849	896	34	31	43

* Led league   ** Season ended by player strike August 11
I Selected by Orioles in June 1978 free agent draft (2nd round Baltimore's 4th selection)

ALL-STAR		AVG	G	AB	R	H	2B	3B	HR	RBI	BB	SO	SB	CS	HP
1983	AL at Chi	.000	1	0	0	0	0	0	0	0	1	0	0	0	0
1984	AL at SF	.000	1	0	0	0	0	0	0	0	0	0	0	0	0
1985	AL at Minn	.333	1	3	0	1	0	0	0	0	0	0	0	0	0
1986	AL at Hou	.000	1	4	0	0	0	0	0	0	0	0	0	0	0
1987	AL at Oak	.500	1	2	0	1	0	0	0	0	0	0	0	0	0
1988	AL at Cin	.000	1	3	0	0	0	0	0	0	1	0	0	0	0
1989	AL at Cal	.333	1	3	0	1	0	0	0	0	0	0	0	0	0
1990	AL at Chi	.000	1	2	0	0	0	0	0	0	0	0	0	0	0
1991	AL at Tor	.667	1	3	1	2	0	0	1	3	0	0	0	0	0
1992	AL at SD	.333	1	3	0	1	0	0	0	1	0	0	0	0	0
1993	AL at Bal	.000	1	3	0	0	0	0	0	0	0	1	0	0	0
1994	AL at Pitt	.200	1	5	0	1	1	0	0	0	0	2	0	0	0
Totals		.226	11	31	1	7	1	0	1	4	2	3	0	0	0

ALCS		AVG	G	AB	R	H	2B	3B	HR	RBI	BB	SO	SB	CS	HP
1983	Bal vs. Chi	.400	4	15	5	6	2	0	0	1	2	3	0	0	1

WORLD SERIES		AVG	G	AB	R	H	2B	3B	HR	RBI	BB	SO	SB	CS	HP
1983	Bal vs. Phi	.167	5	18	2	3	0	0	0	1	3	4	0	0	0

KEY

G games played	**H** hits	**HR** home runs	**SO** strikeouts	**CS** caught stealing
AB at bats	**2B** doubles	**RBI** runs batted in	**SB** stolen bases	**HP** hit by pitch
R runs scored	**3B** triples	**BB** bases on balls		

INDEX

Index